Keep Going, Don't Give Up

VANECIA CODNER

For permission requests, contact:
Purpose Publishing via email at contactus@purposepublishing.com.

Printed in the United States of America

Paperback ISBN: 978-1-965319-50-5

Purpose Publishing LLC.
13194 US Highway 301 South
Suite 417
Riverview, Florida 33578

www.PurposePublishing.com

Acknowledgments

James 1:2-3 (NIV) – Consider it pure joy, my brothers and sisters, whenever you face trials of many kinds, because you know that the testing of your faith produces perseverance.

I want to thank God first for giving me this vision. My prayer is that this devotional will heal hearts and lift spirits. I hope it encourages those struggling with grief to find solace in a way that glorifies God.

To my husband, Domingo, and my children, Alex and Za'Nyla, thank you for your love and support during this season of my life. You all encourage me in ways that I can't express in words. I love you more than you will ever know.

With heartfelt gratitude, I acknowledge every person who offered their insights, expertise, and encouragement in any form or fashion along this journey. Your support has been a guiding light in bringing this book to completion.

Special Acknowledgement

To my dear Za'Nyla, your health journey and the close brush with losing you tested my faith profoundly. Your journey has transformed my life, teaching me that our pain holds purpose, and without it, there can be no growth. Thank you for your incredible resilience.

This devotional was inspired by my loved ones, whom I miss every day.

> *John 16:22 (NIV) – So, with you: Now is your time of grief, but I will see you again and you will rejoice, and no one will take away your joy.*

In Loving Memory of

Aaron Lindsay (Paternal Grandfather)
Sunrise: May 29, 1932 - Sunset: November 6, 2021

Vincent Otis Lindsay II (Brother)
Sunrise: July 25, 1987 - Sunset: December 19, 2021

Gertrude McCoy (Maternal Grandmother)
Sunrise: February 24, 1943 - Sunset: July 22, 2022

Vincent Otis Lindsay (Father)
Sunrise: December 20, 1961 - Sunset: November 26, 2022

Encouragement

When going through life, it is easy to lose yourself as you go through the difficulties that life throws at us.

When we are going through the ups, life is good. Usually, we are happy. Family is good, our job is going well, and we can make money for ourselves or our families. We have good friends that surround us, a family that loves us, we eat well; we have a home and a roof over our heads, and life is good. One, two, all, or some may apply to you, but either way, you're feeling good about where you are in life.

When we are going through our downs, we may experience different emotions. Sadness, anger, depression, anxiety, stress, or grieving the loss of a loved one, a job, a relationship, a pet, and many more.

The good news is that these big feelings that we are experiencing are normal; you are normal. We all have experienced some or all of these feelings at some point in our lives. When we have these feelings, it's important that we trust God through the process. Trust that God can and will bring us out of sadness and bring us joy through whatever is making us sad. Trust God and know that when we are angry, depressed, and feeling anxious that the Enemy has now come in and taken over and know that we need to lean on God to see us through.

Romans 15:13 (NIV) says, "May the God of hope fill you with all joy and peace as you trust in him, so that you may overflow with hope by the power of the Holy Spirit."

"Trusting in God does not mean we are immune to negative feelings. Rather, it means we have hope that God will fill us with joy and peace. Through wholehearted trust in God, we can persevere through our challenges. As Proverbs 3:5-6 (NKJV) advises, 'Trust in the LORD with all your heart, and lean not on your own understanding; In all your ways acknowledge Him, And He shall direct your paths.'"

Do not let the Enemy steal your joy. Do not succumb to sitting in anger, depression, anxiety, and grief, feeling as though there is no way out—that is a lie. There's a familiar saying: "There is light at the end of the tunnel." When you find yourself enveloped in darkness, remember that God is rooting for you. You've got this; you can do it. If you give up, you may never gain clarity, but if you persist, God will guide you through. God embodies love, and as 1 Corinthians 13:7 (NIV) states, "Love always protects, always trusts, always hopes, always perseveres."

God's love is both the means and the motivation for you to maintain hope. When you feel rejected, God will instill hope within you. Your darkest days are not the conclusion of your story; rather, I believe they mark the beginning. We look forward to a better future with the help and guidance of

God. A love that always perseveres is one that never gives up. John 15:12 (NIV) instructs us, "This is my commandment: Love each other as I have loved you." Even when you have given up on Him, God never gives up on you—His love remains steadfast.

My Story

In the span of one year, I endured the loss of four people who were incredibly close to my heart: my paternal grandfather, my younger brother, my maternal grandmother, and my father. Not even a year had passed when my daughter faced a life-threatening illness. She was diagnosed with acute respiratory failure, Influenza B, and MRSA (Methicillin-Resistant Staphylococcus Aureus) bacterial pneumonia, leaving her in critical condition for 34 days in the Pediatric Intensive Care Unit (PICU) at our local children's hospital. She experienced profound hypoxia and struggled to breathe, necessitating the use of a ventilator for 15 days. Due to the high-flow ventilation, she developed air leak syndrome and required Extracorporeal Membrane Oxygenation (ECMO) for 24 days. During this harrowing time, she had to be resuscitated three times. We were uncertain of whether she would survive.

At this point, my faith was truly tested. It was an experience unlike any I had known before, filled with immense sadness, something that seemed much larger than myself, overwhelming to face alone.

Raised in the church, my relationship with God hasn't always been close. However, losing four dearly loved ones and my daughter's near-death experience drove me to prayer, to lean on God for support through these excruciatingly difficult times. I prayed for comfort and strength. As my daughter battled her illness, I pleaded with God, "Please heal my daughter. Let her make it through this." Yet, a voice inside me whispered doubts about her survival. It made me question my trust in God. Would I be angry with Him if she passed away? If death were the outcome, it would mean God hadn't responded to my prayers in the way I had hoped. Eventually, I altered my prayers, accepting His will: "I trust Your plan, God. Whatever Your plan is for my daughter, I trust it, for Your plan is perfect." There were moments when words failed me, and I had to rely on the prayers of others.

Before my daughter fell ill, my husband was a tremendous support, taking on the roles of caregiver for our children, cook, cleaner, and caretaker of our home, as I was often away caring for my loved ones. When our daughter became sick, he fully embraced fatherhood for our son, while I spent most of my time in the PICU with our daughter. Our life as we knew it was temporarily altered. My husband became the pillar that held us together. He would frequently cite the Bible verse James 1:6-8 (KJV): "But let him ask in faith, nothing wavering. For he that wavereth is like a wave of the sea driven with the wind and tossed. For let not that man think that he shall receive any thing of the Lord. A double minded man is unstable in all his ways." This verse serves as a reminder to maintain our faith. Regardless of our circumstances, we must remember that God is always with us. Echoing the words of our late grandfather, "All is well," we hold on to this assurance through both the good times and the challenging times.

During these challenging times, family and friends reached out through phone calls, text messages, and social media, all expressing their sympathy. Many said, "I am praying for you." Somehow, I began to feel the comfort and strength that God promises when we place our trust in Him. An inexplicable shift occurred in my life. Fully trusting in God was the best decision I could have made—it transformed me. Unexpectedly, through the loss of my loved ones and my daughter's brush with death, my relationship with God improved, which, in turn, made me a better person. It made me a better wife, daughter, sister, friend—overall, a better human being. The lesson I learned through loss and heartache is to trust in God. When we do, He will provide comfort and a strength unlike any we've known before.

Despite experiencing great loss, I have become the best version of myself thus far. I am grateful to God for His knowledge, wisdom, and understanding. Having been surrounded by Christianity all my life, it was only recently that I truly developed a relationship with God. This relationship has allowed me to see more clearly, hear from God more frequently and distinctly, and become more protective of the people in my life, as well as more discerning of what I hear and see. Prior to this relationship, it was challenging to discern who or what had my best interests at heart. Making sound judgments about my actions or the company I kept was difficult. It was tough to determine whether the people in my life were adding value or merely draining my time and energy. Now, with a closer relationship to God, He grants me discernment in all my endeavors, enabling me to differentiate between what is morally and spiritually right or wrong according to His teachings. Bible study tools describe discernment as often associated with wisdom, understanding, and insight, and considered a gift of the Holy Spirit. CRU. org explains:

> "The presence of the Holy Spirit in your life changes everything about hearing God's voice. If you have chosen to begin a personal relationship with Jesus, His Spirit now lives within you. So rather than wondering where God is and how to connect with Him, you can have complete confidence that He lives within you and is always ready to guide you. If you have not yet invited Jesus into your life, find out how you can know God personally. God speaks to you through the Bible. In it, God tells you how to live the life He has called you to live. The Bible is full of stories with lessons, stories with God speaking truth and God revealing what you need to hear to lead a life that blesses Him. God also speaks through the internal promptings of the Holy Spirit. John 14:26 says that the Spirit teaches you and helps you remember what God has done. The Holy Spirit prompts you to act in obedience, to turn away from sinful things, and to reach out to the people around you for support. Internal promptings can urge you to share the message of Jesus with the people in your life. Find out more about the Holy Spirit and how you can experience more of God in your life. God wants to make His

voice known to you. He has no desire to confuse you. The combination of His Spirit within you and His living word, the Bible, in front of you is His plan for teaching you to recognize His voice. So why do many Christians live their lives wondering exactly what God is saying or whether He is still speaking at all? The answer may lie in understanding what distracts you from hearing God.

"John 16:12-15 (NIV) 'I have much more to say to you, more than you can now bear. But when He, the Spirit of truth, comes, He will guide you into all the truth. He will not speak on His own; He will speak only what He hears, and He will tell you what is yet to come. He will glorify Me because it is from Me that He will receive what He will make known to you. All that belongs to the Father is Mine. That is why I said the Spirit will receive from Me that He will make known to you.'"

Despite not fully understanding how, I managed to keep a smile on my face through it all. I was able to comfort and encourage those around me, even while grieving myself. I remained a good wife to my husband and a great mother to my children. I could feel God's presence and witnessed His promises being kept. This doesn't mean I'm without moments of sadness—quite the opposite. Over time, my grief seemed to intensify, especially during moments that reminded me of my loved ones. Passing places that brought memories of them would often bring me to tears. While cooking, I'd sometimes cry, recalling the times I needed advice on meals or specific dishes, when I could easily call my dad or expect his nightly calls. The realization that I could no longer make those calls was heartbreaking. Sewing would remind me of my grandmother, an amazing quilter who taught me the craft. My little brother's calls for advice, or his need for a ride to work, echoed the love my grandfather showed me and my family. He was a man I could always rely on for wisdom—the true definition of love.

As my grief intensified, I called upon God, and His presence became increasingly palpable. Strength is not the absence of sadness or grief; rather, it signifies that in those moments, we do not dwell in sorrow or allow the Adversary to lead us into stress or depression. Instead, we place our trust in God to guide us through. Despite not understanding why, I suddenly felt a sense of peace, even though I had lost many close to me in a short span and had seen my daughter endure a traumatic event. The more I sought and trusted in God, the clearer His voice became to me, and I sensed that He was leading me to my true calling, which is Love—being a genuine embodiment of love. Through loving and obeying God, I discovered my identity by placing my trust in Him. On the journey of self-discovery, it is crucial to pray and seek God first.

I WILL NOT COMPARE MYSELF TO OTHER PEOPLE.

2 Corinthians 10:12 (NIV) – We do not dare to classify or compare ourselves with some who commend themselves. When they measure themselves by themselves and compare themselves with themselves, they are not wise.

It's important that we avoid comparing ourselves to others. Why? Because such comparisons can lead to unhappiness, jealousy, and low self-esteem, among other negative feelings. In the age of social media, we're granted a glimpse into the lives of others—celebrities, the wealthy, the less fortunate, old friends, new friends, coworkers, and even those we may not particularly like. Yet, often, we don't truly know these individuals. They might be people we've met in passing, from elementary school, middle school, high school, or college. We might follow them because they run a business we're interested in. Regardless, we frequently find ourselves disconnected from them, sometimes having never connected at all.

The danger lies in comparing our lives to theirs, which may not even reflect reality. We see only what is presented—a curated display of lavish vacations, career achievements, perfect family moments, or exquisite meals. But we don't see the struggles, the pain, or the hard work behind these seemingly perfect snapshots.

God created each of us uniquely, with our own literal fingerprints. Scripture, specifically 2 Corinthians 10:12, advises against comparing ourselves to others, noting it is unwise. Such behavior is unhealthy. Instead, we should focus on self-improvement and confidence-building. By working diligently towards our goals and seeking to understand God's purpose for us, we can find fulfillment. Keep persevering and never give up!

I WILL NOT WORRY ABOUT WHAT OTHER PEOPLE THINK ABOUT ME.

Galatians 1:10 (NIV) – Am I now trying to win the approval of human beings, or of God? Or am I trying to please people? If I were still trying to please people, I would not be a servant of Christ.

It's hard not to worry about what others think of you; we've all been guilty of this at some point. Galatians 1:10 poses a question: "Am I now trying to win the approval of humans, or of God? Or am I trying to please people? If I were still trying to please people, I would not be a servant of Christ." Therefore, I encourage you to consider whose approval you're truly seeking. Is it your significant other, your family, your close friends, social media, your job, or your colleagues? Who is it that you think of when you wake up, desiring to look good for them, to perform excellently to gain their praise? Sometimes, it's not a conscious thought, but subconsciously, we all seek approval from someone in this world, in one way or another. It's a normal feeling, but it can become unhealthy if we don't prioritize seeking God's favor first. It's crucial to focus on our God-given gifts and use them to glorify God. We shouldn't worry about worldly opinions but seek to please God, for we are servants of Christ, not of the world. Joshua 1:9 (NIV) reminds us, "Have I not commanded you? Be strong and courageous. Do not be afraid; do not be discouraged, for the Lord your God will be with you wherever you go." Keep going and don't give up!

It's okay for me to make mistakes.

Romans 3:23 (NIV) – For all have sinned and fall short of the glory of God.

*R*omans 3:23 reminds us that we are human and prone to error. It's vital to remember that God is forgiving, and when we err, we should seek His forgiveness. "If we confess our sins, He is faithful and just and will forgive us our sins and purify us from all unrighteousness" (1 John 1:9, NIV). Honesty about our mistakes is also crucial. The Bible instructs us to confess our sins to one another and pray for each other. For instance, during my prayer time, I not only approach God for myself but also pray daily for my husband, my children, close family, friends, and global events, among others. We ought to seek forgiveness when we have wronged others, acknowledge our wrongdoings, and ask for forgiveness. The aim is to endeavor to do better moving forward.

Forgiveness is for oneself. I've learned that when I withhold forgiveness, I am the one who suffers. The person I'm upset with has moved on, living what seems to be a happy life, while I remain miserable. Ephesians 4:31-32 advises, "Get rid of all bitterness, rage, and anger, brawling and slander, along with every form of malice. Be kind and compassionate to one another, forgiving each other, just as in Christ God forgave you."

When you are on a journey to become a better version of yourself, you may encounter moments where you feel like a failure or believe you are not good enough. This is a falsehood. You are not a failure; you are sufficient, regardless of the Adversary's attempts to convince you otherwise. No one is flawless; we all falter at times. Making mistakes is a normal part of life, and some errors may have greater consequences than others. Remember, as you strive to improve and encounter setbacks, it is crucial to consult the Bible for guidance through your struggles. The beauty of God's grace is that He can transform any mistake you make and any pain you endure into something beneficial. Through your trials and errors, by placing your trust in God, you will emerge as the best version of yourself. Persist on your journey and never surrender.

I AM MORE THAN WHAT I LOOK LIKE ON THE OUTSIDE.

1 Peter 3:3-4 (NIV) – Your beauty should not come from outward adornment, such as elaborate hairstyles and the wearing of gold jewelry or fine clothes. Rather, it should be that of your inner self, the unfading beauty of a gentle and quiet spirit, which is of great worth in God's sight.

Don't fixate on your external appearance; it can change in an instant. It's more important to focus on your inner well-being—mentally, physically, and spiritually.

Consider these questions: Is your heart in the right place? Are you extending love to others as God loves you, even when it's challenging? Are you offering kindness in a world that can be hateful? Reflect on your health: Are you eating well, exercising, and staying hydrated? How is your mental health? Do you surround yourself with people who genuinely care for you and uplift you? Above all, how is your relationship with God? Are you trusting in Him through every season, especially the tough times?

Working on our inner selves ensures that our outer selves will radiate beauty. Your speech, your demeanor, and your life will shine brightly. You are so much more than your appearance. The state of your mind, body, and spirit is reflected outwardly. There's a saying I've known since childhood: 'When you look good, you feel good.' However, I believe it should be 'When you feel good, you look good.' Maintain a healthy diet, exercise, hydrate, and take care of your mental health, and your body will show it. Reflect on these questions, whether one or all; we all have room for improvement. You're not alone. Turn to God for assistance; we cannot do it alone. We need accountability partners—be it a spouse, family, or friends—who will support and hold us accountable. Remember, you are more than your outward appearance. Keep going and don't give up!

I WILL NOT BE AFRAID TO LET GO OF TOXIC THINGS AND PEOPLE IN MY LIFE.

1 Corinthians 15:33 (KJV) – *Be not deceived: evil communications corrupt good manners.*

Do not let the company you keep mislead you, especially if they bring ill intentions. They may also have good intentions, but still may not be the right companions for your new journey. Whether we acknowledge it or not, we are shaped by those around us. It's crucial to be in the company of good people who genuinely care for us—those who will pray for us, encourage us, and contribute positively to our lives.

Often, there are individuals in our lives who negatively influence our morality and decision-making, and frequently, these are our own family members or those we consider friends. 1 Corinthians 15:33 (KJV) warns, "Be not deceived: evil communications corrupt good manners." This serves as a reminder to be wary of poor company, as it is human nature to emulate the behavior of those with whom we spend the most time.

Recognizing someone as bad company does not necessitate disliking them; rather, it's about being mindful of the time you spend together. Continue to love and encourage them, showing the same kindness and patience that God shows you.

Moreover, be cautious around those who may draw out traits you're striving to leave behind. They might not understand your journey towards change. Familiarity with you from last year, or even last month, doesn't mean they know the person you are now or the one you aim to become. Treat them with love and kindness, recognizing that they may not grasp your path. Growth necessitates change, and it may mean spending less time with certain people or altering your habits. This can be uncomfortable, but have faith that God is cheering you on and has incredible plans for you if you continue to trust in Him. Keep moving forward and never give up!

I WILL NOT LET FEAR HOLD ME BACK FROM PURPOSE.

Isaiah 41:10 (NIV) – *So do not fear for I am with you; do not be dismayed for I am your God. I will strengthen you and help you; I will uphold you with my righteous right hand.*

Fear can only hold you back if you allow it! I have great news for you: you can take control of how fear impacts your life. Yes, I know it's easier said than done, but you can conquer your fear by trusting that God will strengthen you throughout the process. There is something incredibly powerful in the promise that God will fortify you amid fears of the unknown or the evils that surround us daily. There is nothing God cannot do. In every situation, God will provide strength when you place your trust in Him. When we fear the unseen, it indicates a lack of trust in God. We should not let external factors control our thoughts, minds, and actions. Instead, we should trust in the Lord with all our hearts. Fear will undermine your purpose if you permit it.

More great news: You were born with a purpose. God knew exactly what He was doing from the moment you were in your mother's womb. Psalm 139:13-16 (NIV) states:

> "For you created my innermost being
> you knit me together in my mother's

womb. I praise you because I am fearfully and wonderfully made; your works are wonderful; I know that full well. My frame was not hidden from you when I was made in a secret place. When I was woven together in the depths of the earth, your eyes saw my unformed body. All the days ordained for me were written in your book before one of them came to be."

Don't give up! There is a reason you are here, still standing. There is a reason you woke up this morning with the breath of life. It may be that your purpose on this Earth has not yet been fulfilled, or perhaps you have fulfilled it, but you still have something valuable to contribute to the world. If you haven't discovered your purpose and how you can use your gift to help others and glorify God, I encourage you to pray and seek God's wisdom and understanding. To truly hear from God, it's important to cultivate a relationship with Him, to hear and see clearly. Keep going and don't give up!

I WILL TRUST THAT I CAN MAKE GOOD DECISIONS FOR MYSELF.

Psalm 25:4-7 (NIV) – Show me your ways, Lord, teach me your paths. Guide me in your truth and teach me, for you are God my Savior, and my hope is in you all day long. Remember, Lord, your great mercy and love, for they are from old. Do not remember the sins of my youth and my rebellious ways; according to your love remember me, for you, Lord, are good.

Coming from a past filled with poor choices, it can be challenging to trust in your own decision-making. The good news is that having God by your side, walking hand in hand, cheering and rooting for you, makes the journey much easier! Don't attempt it alone. God is with you. Trust in the Lord with all your heart, and He will guide you through.

The important thing to remember is that the mind is incredibly powerful! Continually reassure yourself that you are capable. Affirm, "I can and will make good decisions," and truly believe it. The moment you doubt your ability to make sound choices, you set yourself up for failure. If you tell yourself you can't succeed, then you won't. If you label yourself a failure, you'll live up to that expectation. The power of the mind is often underestimated.

View your past mistakes as opportunities for growth, as lessons intentionally designed by God to help you evolve into a better version of yourself.

Yes, you may have made poor decisions, but those do not define you. Such mistakes can serve as catalysts for personal growth. God desires you to become a better person. We can trust Him at all times. Although we may not fully comprehend God's plan for us, He is dedicated to our ultimate happiness. Cling to God's promises, and He will support you through difficult times. Keep going and don't give up!

I WILL SEEK WISDOM TO STAY ON THE RIGHT PATH.

Ephesians 5:15-17 (NIV) – *Be careful,
then, how you live-not as unwise but as
wise, making the most of every opportunity,
because the days are evil. Therefore, do not
be foolish but understand what the Lord's
will is.*

In a world rife with malevolence, God beckons us to follow
His divine navigation, ensuring we remain on the righteous
path and make prudent decisions, even as adversaries strive
to derail us. God has charted the course from inception to
culmination; our task is to seek wisdom to navigate this
odyssey sagaciously. The steps to wisdom are as follows:

- **Fear God**: Proverbs 9:10 (NIV) teaches that "the
  fear of the Lord is the beginning of wisdom, and
  knowledge of the Holy One is understanding."
- **Desire Wisdom**: Proverbs 2:2-6 (NIV) encourages
  us to "turn your ear to wisdom and apply your heart
  to understanding… then you will understand the
  fear of the Lord and find the knowledge of God.
  For the Lord gives wisdom; from His mouth come
  knowledge and understanding."
- **Pray for Wisdom**: James 1:5-8 (NIV) advises, "If
  any of you lacks wisdom, you should ask God…

But when you ask, you must believe and not doubt…"

- **Study God's Word**: Psalm 19:7-8 extols, "The law of the Lord is perfect, reviving the soul. The statutes of the Lord are trustworthy, making wise the simple."

By adhering to these tenets, we can make wise decisions that align with God's plan for us.

The Adversary's strategy is to derail you with distractions, leading to a destructive path. Once on this path, you may face torment from depression, anxiety, and the profound grief of losing loved ones, among other trials. Fighting this battle alone is futile; without support, you'll find yourself trapped in darkness, facing insurmountable obstacles. This bleak road is not what God has ordained for you. Be vigilant against the snares of the Enemy. The only way to realign with the right path is through God—this is not a journey to undertake solo. Ephesians 6:10-11 (NIV) encourages us: "Finally, be strong in the Lord and in His mighty power. Put on the full armor of God so that you can take your stand against the devil's schemes." Trust in God's plan, stay the course He has set for you, and you will find your reward. Keep going and never give up!

I WILL PUT GOD FIRST
IN ALL THAT I DO.

*Matthew 6:33 (KJV) – But seek ye first the
kingdom of God and his righteousness and
all these things shall be added unto you.*

As believers in Christ, we hold that God is our utmost priority. To non-believers, this concept may seem irrational. However, I encourage you to give it a chance! Place God first in everything you do, believe with all your heart that God loves you, desires the best for you, and trust that things can and will improve.

Observe the changes God brings into your life. Will everything be perfect? No, for we still face temptations from the Enemy that bring us down and stir anxiety about the world's sins. Genesis Chapter 3 discusses the fall of man, marking the onset of sin. Initially, the world was created in a state of perfection. Silverdale Baptist Academy offers an explanation:

> "God created the world for good, and He created humans to do good. However, He also gave humans the ability to choose, known as free will. This means that even though humans were created to do good, they can also choose to do the opposite of good, what we have

termed evil. We cannot blame God when humans choose to do the opposite of that which they were created to do. Therefore, why did God create humans with free will? He did it so that humans could love Him and each other. If humans had no choice but to love God and each other, then that wouldn't really mean very much at all. Humans would just be little robots performing the action they were programmed to do. However, since humans have the choice to either love or not love, it truly is love that is conveyed when humans choose to love God or each other. Therefore, it would be impossible and illogical for a world to exist in which humans with free will exist without the potential for evil. The very existence of free will produces the potential for good and for the opposite of good. If you haven't already put God first, it will change your life!"

Keep going! Don't give up!

It's Okay for Me to Feel My Pain Fully.

2 Corinthians 1:3-4 (NIV) – Praise be to the God and Father of our Lord Jesus Christ, the Father of compassion and the God of all comfort, who comforts us in all our troubles so that we can comfort those in any trouble with the comfort we ourselves have received from God.

Stop and breathe! Everything is going to be okay. Scripture reassures us that we serve a God of compassion, the God of all comfort, who comforts us in all our troubles. When we face challenges, God is with us. We need only to call on Him and trust that He will assist us. God accompanies us through everything and will provide comfort during our trials.

When I lost four loved ones in one year, I initially felt numb. As time passed and the reality set in that they were no longer with me, the pain surfaced, and I would find myself crying. At times, I felt guilty for my grief, questioning why I was so deeply hurt. I do trust God, and I understand that things happen for a reason. Yet, the truth remains that trusting God doesn't diminish the fact that I miss my loved ones immensely, and it's okay to feel an overwhelming sense of sadness.

The most crucial lesson is not to dwell in sadness for too long. The longer I lingered in it, the deeper the sadness became.

The Adversary is adept at finding our vulnerabilities and keeping us down. He knows how to incite anxiety, leading to a creeping sense of depression, where hours of hurt turn into days, then weeks, and even years. It can be challenging to regain composure, as if trapped in a dark place with no escape. This despair can affect not only you but also those you love. That's why, at the first sign of sadness, anxiety, depression, or grief, we must turn to God without delay. Pray and seek God's presence; do not allow the Enemy any opportunity to infiltrate. Pain is a natural emotion, but it's important not to remain in that state. Keep moving forward and never give up!

It's okay for me to enjoy the remarkable things that are happening in my life.

John 10:10 (KJV) – *The thief cometh not,*
but for to steal, and to kill, and to destroy;
I come that they might have life, and that
they might have it more abundantly.

It is perfectly fine to relish life and the blessings God bestows upon you. Contrary to the myth that Christianity is dull and restrictive, the truth is far from it. Scripture declares in John 10:10 (KJV), "The thief cometh not, but for to steal, and to kill, and to destroy: I am come that they might have life, and that they might have it more abundantly." These words from Jesus affirm that He desires for us (you and me) to live life to the fullest.

"Abundantly" implies a life rich and overflowing with joy. God wishes for us to take pleasure in life, but through a biblical lens. When you foster a relationship with God, He elevates your enjoyment to new heights, revealing wonders unseen and experiences unknown, filling your life with smiles and laughter. I can attest to this, having found joy both secularly and through a biblical perspective. 1 Timothy 6:17 (KJV) advises, "Charge them that are rich in this world, that they be not highminded, nor trust in uncertain riches, but in the living God, who giveth us richly all things to enjoy." While worldly wealth is transient, God generously provides all we need for our joy. Trust in the Lord with all your heart, and you cannot err. The deeper our trust in the Lord and the closer our relationship with Him, the more we will savor life and the gifts He has granted us in abundance. Keep going and never give up!

I WILL UNDERSTAND MY GOD-GIVEN GIFT.

1 Peter 4:10 (NIV) – Each of you should use whatever gift you have received to serve others, as faithful stewards of God's grace in its various forms.

What is your gift? If you're still exploring what your gift is and your purpose in God's kingdom, consider these questions: What ignites your passion? What activities bring you joy? What are you skilled at? What bothers you when it's not done correctly?

God has endowed each of us with a gift, and it's our duty to use that gift to honor God and serve His kingdom. Our aim should be to employ our gifts to assist others. James 1:17 (NIV) states, "Every good and perfect gift is from above, coming down from the Father of the heavenly lights, who does not change like shifting shadows." We are each blessed with distinct gifts. What I excel at may not be your forte, and vice versa, but all contribute significantly to God's kingdom. Your gift is an innate talent, a unique skill or ability that comes naturally, not through learning. While we can always enhance and refine our gifts, they are inherent qualities that distinguish us from others. As my mentor once advised:

> "Believe in your ability to realize your
> gift. Abide by the laws that safeguard

it. Strategize your approach towards nurturing your gift. Surround yourself with supportive people and be wary of those who may stifle or harm your gift. Persist and manage the pressures from naysayers as you employ your gift. Pray over your gift daily, seeking guidance for your purpose and role in God's kingdom. Ask for clarity in defining it and for God's help in keeping it vibrant. Lastly, share your gift with the world. Don't aim to profit from it initially; instead, volunteer your gift as a service to others. When we freely offer our gifts, everything else will naturally follow."

1 Peter 4:10-11 (NIV) instructs us: "Each of you should use whatever gift you have received to serve others, as faithful stewards of God's grace in its various forms. If anyone speaks, they should do so as one who speaks the very words of God. If anyone serves, they should do so with the strength God provides, so that in all things God may be praised through Jesus Christ. To Him be the glory and the power forever and ever. Amen." Keep going and don't give up!

I WILL DESIRE GREATNESS.

Philippians 4:13 (KJV) – I can do all things through Christ which strengtheneth me.

Do you truly aspire to greatness? Do you wish to be the best version of yourself, the person God intends you to be? The answer is a resounding yes! We all yearn for greatness. Yet, what defines greatness? Often, we measure it by our successes: popularity, social media followers, prosperous businesses, wealth, luxurious possessions, and a picture-perfect family. These are commonly seen as symbols of success and greatness. While there's nothing inherently wrong with these achievements, biblical teachings offer a different perspective on greatness.

True greatness is defined by how we serve others to glorify God and humble ourselves. As the familiar adage goes, "Treat others as you would like to be treated." No one wishes to be mistreated. Matthew 25:31-46 echoes this sentiment, teaching us that our actions towards others reflect our service to God. By serving others, we honor God and bring glory to Him.

So, do you earnestly seek greatness? If you're unsure, that's okay. Strive for greatness by serving others with the gifts God has given you. In doing so, God will bless you for blessing others, and you will achieve true greatness. Keep going and never give up!

I WILL BE KIND TO MYSELF.

3 John 1:2 (NIV) – Dear friend, I pray that you may enjoy good health and that all may go well with you, even as your soul is getting along well.

Life can be challenging, presenting us with numerous reasons to feel upset or unhappy, and sometimes we're harsh on ourselves. But it's okay! Your current struggles or past experiences do not define you. You will persevere!

Life is akin to a rollercoaster, complete with its ups and downs, twists and turns, smooth and rough patches, followed by more challenges until the journey concludes. Just like life, you must keep moving forward. Don't give up and don't abandon the ride. Only God determines when the ride is over. Along the way, you won't get everything right—none of us do.

Remember, you are not alone. If you feel isolated, know that you have a friend in Jesus. To those who may be skeptical, it might seem implausible, but I encourage you to give faith a chance.

> John 15:15 (NIV) says, "I no longer call you servants, because a servant does not know his master's business. Instead, I have called you friends, for everything

that I learned from my Father I have made known to you."

Jesus invites us to know Him, promising the key to unlock the door to the Father. This implies that without a friendship with Jesus, one may not perceive God's guidance clearly. However, once a relationship with Jesus Christ is established, clarity emerges. You begin to view the world through a new lens.

In times of trouble, God endows you with what I like to call "superpowers," enabling you to overcome any challenge the Adversary presents. You are enveloped in an overwhelming sense of comfort and strength to confront any situation. God illuminates solutions and dispels confusion, granting you true peace. This doesn't mean problems vanish; rather, it signifies that when difficulties or grief arise, you handle them differently than you would without Jesus as your ally. Be gentle with yourself. You've come this far. Keep going and don't give up!

I WILL SHOW KINDNESS
TO OTHER PEOPLE.

*Luke 6:35 – But love ye your enemies,
and do good, and lend, hoping for nothing
again; and your reward shall be great, and
ye shall be the children of the Highest: for
he is kind unto the unthankful and to evil.*

People don't always make it easy to show kindness. The world is often filled with hate, which can make being kind challenging. However, we never truly know what others are enduring. A simple act of kindness can go a long way.

What does kindness mean? According to the Oxford Dictionary, it is the quality of being friendly, generous, and considerate. The Merriam-Webster Dictionary defines it as having a sympathetic or helpful nature. It also encompasses gentleness, compassion, and affection. Kindness is a sincere sentiment that emanates from the heart. When you display genuine kindness, it is done without regret, and it feels rewarding to be kind to others.

Has there ever been a time when you were struggling or simply having a tough day? We can all answer "yes" to that question. We all face challenges and have bad days. During such times, has anyone ever shown you kindness? Whether it's an act that lifts your spirits, a favorite treat, or a cherished gift. Perhaps someone offered encouraging words, made you laugh, and brightened your day. These are all meaningful ways to demonstrate kindness that can have a lasting impact.

Have you been kind to others? If not, it's never too late! It's crucial to treat people as you would like to be treated. The Bible speaks of God's kindness toward us and how we should extend kindness to others. It may be difficult to be kind if you feel the world has been unkind to you, but rest assured that God will reward your acts of kindness without expecting anything in return. Galatians 6:9 encourages us, "And let us not grow weary of doing good, for in due season we will reap if we do not give up." Your time will come, but if you give up, you'll miss the opportunity to experience the remarkable blessings God has planned for you. Keep going and don't give up!

I WILL SHOW LOVE IN ALL THAT I DO.

1 Corinthians 13:4-8 (NIV) – Love is patient, love is kind. It does not envy, it does not boast, it is not proud. It does not dishonor others, it is not self-seeking, it is not easily angered, it keeps no record of wrongs. Love does not delight in evil but rejoices with the truth. It always protects, always trusts, always hopes, always perseveres. Love never fails. But where there are prophecies, they will cease; where there are tongues, they will be stilled; where there is knowledge, it will pass away.

Show love in all that you do! You don't need to agree with someone's lifestyle to love them or show love. It's possible to disagree with others' views and still love them. The Bible teaches that faith without love is empty. Love always protects, trusts, hopes, and perseveres. Love never fails.

Consider the people you love most; they may have flaws or struggles, but you still love, respect, and wish the best for them. As Christians, we pray for them. You might share these struggles, yet those around you still offer love, kindness, and respect.

1 Corinthians 13:4-13 details how we should love: with patience, kindness, without envy, humbly, without rudeness

or selfishness, not easily angered, forgiving, and rejoicing in truth. I encourage you to spread love, even when it's challenging, even when you disagree with someone's choices. Love never fails.

I WILL TRUST GOD IN ALL THAT I DO.

Proverbs 3:5-6 (NIV) – Trust in the Lord with all thine heart and lean not unto thine own understanding. In all thy ways acknowledge him, and he shall direct thy paths.

Imagine someone knowing your every move. Picture a Being who has been aware of your entire life even before your birth. They know the moment you will enter this world and when you will draw your last breath. They understand everything about you, both internally and externally. They crafted a unique fingerprint solely for you, one that nobody else in this vast world possesses. They are privy to all your secrets and possess a deeper understanding of you than you have of yourself. When you find yourself alone, they are present to support you and lend an ear. You can be your true self around them. They already recognize you, for they are the Creator.

All that is required of you is to trust in the Lord with all your heart and not rely on your own understanding. In every aspect of your life, acknowledge Him, and He will guide your path. This signifies that if you place your complete trust in the Lord during both prosperous and challenging times, adhere to God's Word, and emulate God's image, He will lead you. Do not attempt to navigate life independently, seeking answers to questions that God already holds. For God knows every thought, word, or action we may conceive.

God calls for acknowledgment. Recognize that He sent His Son to Earth to disseminate the good news of our Heavenly Father. Acknowledge that Jesus sacrificed Himself on the cross for our transgressions so that upon our passing, we may ascend to Heaven and partake in eternal life—a realm devoid of pain and illness. A place where depression, anxiety, sadness, worry, and confusion cease to exist. A place untainted by sin, filled instead with pure joy and happiness. Heaven is a sanctuary of peace, love, community, and worship.

> In John 14:2-3 (KJV) it says, "In My Father's house are many mansions; if it were not so, I would have told you. I will go to prepare a place for you. And if I go and prepare a place for you, I will come again and receive you unto myself; that where I am, there ye may be also."

I have also heard it described as a place of unimaginable blessing. Scripture states that God has already prepared a place for us in Heaven. To reach it, we must trust in God and acknowledge Him, and He will guide us on the path to our eternal home in heaven. Keep going! Don't give up!

I WILL HAVE PATIENCE WITH MYSELF AND OTHER PEOPLE.

Ephesians 4:2 (NIV) – Be completely humble, and gentle; be patient, bearing one another in love.

Take it easy on yourself! Life is challenging, and we all make mistakes, so be gentle with yourself. Whatever you're enduring, you will persevere and emerge on the other side. Remember, you're not alone in your struggles. In fact, there's always someone facing tougher circumstances. It's important to be patient with yourself on this journey and extend that patience to others as we all navigate life.

Patience, whether with oneself or with others, is not a simple concept. In today's world, we crave instant gratification. With the internet, social media, and the approaching era of artificial intelligence, we've grown accustomed to immediate results. A mere click can reveal information about a person, place, or thing. We've become used to having our desires fulfilled promptly. However, our timing isn't always aligned with God's timing.

Psalm 27:14 (NIV) advises, "Wait for the Lord; be strong and take heart and wait for the Lord." God's timing is impeccable—never early, never late. He is always punctual. Ephesians 4:2 (NIV) instructs us to "be completely humble and gentle; be patient, bearing with one another in love."

Remember, God is benevolent. He knows what's best for us, having known us even before our birth. God's love is protective, and He desires the best for us.

Whether you're awaiting a job opportunity, a promotion at work, enduring trials, seeking a life partner, or dealing with unruly children—be patient. Psalm 40:1 (NIV) states, "I waited patiently for the Lord; He turned to me and heard my cry. He lifted me out of the slimy pit, out of the mud and mire; He set my feet on a rock and gave me a firm place to stand."

Cultivate a relationship with God, so that when you seek wisdom, knowledge, and understanding, you can receive clear guidance from Him. Be patient! When you have a relationship with God, patience becomes a cornerstone of your faith.

I WILL SHOW SELF-CONTROL BECAUSE I AM IN CONTROL OF HOW I FEEL.

2 Timothy 1:7 (KJV) – For God hath not given us the spirit of fear; but of power, and of love, and of a sound mind.

It's easy to blame others when we feel out of control. However, we have the power to choose how we respond to situations or individuals that may seem beyond our control or who might have acted rudely towards us. As Proverbs 15:1 states, "A gentle answer turns away wrath, but a harsh word stirs up anger." Consider this: when someone behaves disrespectfully, a soft and gentle reply will often defuse the tension, preventing the situation from escalating further.

There are times when it's crucial to stand up for ourselves, yet it's not just about what we say, but also how we express it. A harsh reaction is likely to exacerbate the conflict. Ephesians 4:26-27 advises, "In your anger do not sin: Do not let the sun go down while you are still angry, and do not give the devil a foothold." This passage is a reminder that feeling anger is a normal human experience. We've all felt it at some point, but managing our anger is key to maintaining control. You can express anger without sinning by responding gently. Avoid giving the Devil an opportunity to influence you in moments of anger.

The aim should always be to de-escalate and soothe the situation as much as possible. Sometimes, the best course of action is to walk away. Don't allow the Enemy any chance to exacerbate your anger. In just a few seconds, you might find yourself saying or doing things you'll regret. The Enemy seeks to disrupt and destroy, but God's plan is to bring peace and improvement. His plan is mighty, always effective, and ultimately triumphant. Keep going! Don't give up!

I WILL PROTECT MY JOY.

Romans 15:13 (NIV) – May the God of hope fill you with all joy and peace as you trust in him, so that you may overflow with hope by the power of the Holy Spirit.

J oy is truly a gift from God! The Oxford Dictionary defines joy as a feeling of intense pleasure and happiness. It's a universal truth that everyone seeks happiness and the experience of joy. This desire is not up for debate. No one yearns to be unhappy, depressed, anxious, or to live in fear or sadness. These negative emotions are not from God. Life may indeed present us with challenges, and the sin or evil of this world may knock on our doors. However, God's greatness surpasses any challenge that the Enemy may throw our way.

Romans 15:13 (NIV) states, "May the God of hope fill you with all joy and peace as you trust in Him." God's desire is to fill us with an abundance of joy and happiness. He encourages us to trust in Him, believe in Him, and promises that He will fill us with hope through the power of the Holy Spirit. This promise has been life-changing. Even during the toughest times, God has a way of providing joy, peace, and happiness, and He can do the same for you.

If your joy doesn't come from the God of hope, then where does it stem from? Is it from people, places, or things of this world? Unfortunately, these worldly aspects can disappoint us. The real question is not if, but when they will let us down, because it's bound to happen eventually.

May the God of hope fill you with *all* joy and peace as you trust in Him, so that you may overflow with hope by the power of the Holy Spirit. The longing for joy, peace in our hearts and minds, and the pursuit of happiness are indisputable. I encourage you to truly get to know God and who He is. Develop a relationship with Him.

I serve a God who loves you and wants nothing but the best for you. He wants you to be filled with joy. Trust in God with all your heart, and He will fill you with joy. Keep going! Never give up!

I WILL PROTECT MY PEACE.

John 14:27 (NIV) – Peace I leave with you;
my peace I give you. I do not give to you as
the world gives. Do not let your heart be
troubled and do not be troubled and do not
be afraid.

How is your peace of mind? How do you manage to protect it? We all struggle with this at some point because evil and sin are rampant in this world every day. True peace comes from God. Thus, we can install locks on our doors to safeguard our peace, preventing anyone from breaking into our homes. We can equip our homes and cars with security systems to help protect our families and the things we invest in. All these measures are beneficial. The world offers many items that we can purchase to help us protect our peace, and there's nothing wrong with any of them.

But what if those measures fail us? What if the locks on our doors don't work? What if our security systems malfunction? Do you still have peace of mind, or do you panic?

The scripture says in John 14:27 (NIV), "Peace I leave with you; my peace I give you." Therefore, God grants us peace, not derived from worldly things we use for protection. That same scripture continues, "I do not give to you as the world gives." Hence, the peace that God provides does not originate from worldly things but from the Holy Spirit. At the end of that scripture, it states, "Do not let your hearts be troubled and do not be afraid." God is assuring us, saying, "*I got you!* Trust in me with all your heart, and I will grant you peace. Even when people or worldly things fail you, *I got you.*"

God is benevolent, and He does not want us to live in fear. God desires our trust in Him and His word, and you will be astonished by the amount of peace you possess. Even in dire situations, God will bestow peace upon you and reassure you through the Holy Spirit that *everything*, not just some things, will be okay.

John 16:33 (NIV) declares, "I have told you these things, so that in me you may have peace. In this world, you will face troubles. But take heart! I have overcome the world." Keep going! Don't give up!

I WILL SURROUND MYSELF
WITH GOOD PEOPLE.

Proverbs 13:20 (NIV) – Walk with the wise and become wise, for a companion of fools suffers harm.

Surround yourself with good people and those who have great ideas. Choose the company of those who make wise decisions, for their wisdom is likely to influence your own choices. Conversely, aligning yourself with individuals who consistently make poor choices can lead you down a similar path.

The decision to improve and make wiser choices can alter the dynamics of existing relationships, especially if those around you do not share your aspirations. It's a common belief that one's environment doesn't impact their actions; however, scripture warns that the company of the unwise can lead to harm. It's important to be in the presence of those who support and encourage you, celebrating your achievements and supporting your journey.

Trust in God's wisdom to bring the right people into your life and to remove those who hinder your growth. Proverbs 13:20 (NIV) advises, "Walk with the wise and become wise, for a companion of fools suffers harm." Comfort in longstanding behaviors, even if foolish, can feel right, but ultimately, they can corrupt good morals, reflected in one's actions, thoughts, and feelings. Growing wiser doesn't necessitate disliking those with differing morals; it may simply mean spending less time with them or loving them from afar. A relationship with God grants the spirit of discernment, aiding in the recognition of the influence of those around us.

I WILL NOT BE CONSUMED BY
THE EVIL OF THE WORLD.

*Lamentations 3:22-23 (NIV) – Because of
the LORD'S great love we are not consumed,
for his compassions never fail. They are new
every morning; great is your faithfulness.*

I t's so easy to be consumed by all the dreadful things that happen in the world: thousands of murders per day, children going missing, corrupt governments, and the list goes on. However, the scripture reassures us that we are not consumed because of the Lord's great love; His compassions never fail. They are new every morning; great is Your faithfulness. The *Mercy City Church at Home with Jesus Daily Devotional* explains this verse perfectly by stating that:

> "Consumed" is an interesting word. It means to be destroyed, but it also means to be used up, spent, exhausted, and depleted. So, when the Word says, we are NOT consumed, God is making a powerful promise to us. Not only is God promising we will never be overcome by anything in this world, but also, that His love for us will never run out. Every day God resets, restores, and refreshes His provision for us. Every day His love flows continuously, and grace is unlimited.

His love and grace are not "new" every morning because His love is constant and unbreakable. Rather, our trust and faith in Him are given reason to be reaffirmed each day. If we just stop and think about Jesus and what He has done for us and what He is still doing for us, how could we not be moved? It's like Christmas morning every day. It is like a fresh start every day. It is like a full tank of hope and mercy every day. The only thing as believers we would ever be overcome and consumed by is His unlimited love for us!"

I appreciate the clarity of their explanation. It all ultimately leads to loving God, trusting in Him, placing our faith in Him, and fostering a relationship with Him. When we embrace these practices, God promises that nothing in this world will ever overwhelm us, and His love will be unending. The peace that God bestows upon us—when the world seeks to engulf us—is beyond words, yet this true and genuine peace is accessible only through God. Keep going! Don't give up!

I WILL NOT FOCUS ON MY PAST BUT WILL FOCUS ON MY FUTURE.

Jeremiah 29:11 (NIV) – For I know the plans I have for you, "declares the Lord," plans to prosper you and not to harm you, plans to give you hope and a future.

Focusing on your past serves only as a distraction from the future that God has envisioned for you. While our past experiences lay the groundwork for our future, it's important not to become mired in them. God has already crafted a plan for you—a plan designed for your prosperity and not for your harm, as stated in Jeremiah 29:11.

If you find yourself ensnared by the hurt, pain, or grief of your past, recognize that this is not the work of God, but that of the Adversary. It's crucial to remember that the Enemy harbors a plan for your life too, aimed at undermining every wonderful thing God intends for you. Without vigilance, the Devil may trap you in a state of despair, convincing you that life holds no further promise or hope. Should you encounter such negative thoughts about the future, reject them—they are falsehoods, and the Enemy is deceitful. God's plan is grander, superior, and it will triumph every time. His design for you is one of flourishing—succeeding in life, fulfilling your purpose, and sharing your God-given gifts with the world. God's intention is to instill hope and to pave the way for a promising future.

If you feel immobilized, turn to prayer and seek God's wisdom, knowledge, understanding, and guidance on how to advance. God does not desire that you linger in the suffering of your past or to remain stagnant. He is already aware of our future, and His timing is impeccable, as is His plan. Rather than dwelling on your past, shift your focus to the future that God has already orchestrated for you. Nurture your relationship with God to gain clarity in hearing and seeing His guidance. It is your duty to seek God's plan and adhere to it, so that you may thrive and avoid the Adversary's intent to lead you astray.

One of the marvelous aspects of God's nature is that He grants us the freedom to choose. You have the option to remain mired in the past, to utter negative declarations over your life, or to heed the deceptions of the Devil. However, I urge you to embrace the plan of God, which carries His promise of prosperity. Place your trust in God's plan and His perfect timing. Do not be ensnared by your history; instead, pursue a relationship with God to fully embrace the life He has designed for you, ensuring you don't miss out on the gifts of joy and peace He bestows.

I encourage you to opt for love and happiness. Choose God over the Devil. Trust in God's plan rather than your own. God is benevolent and seeks only the best for you and your future. I encourage you not to give up, but to keep going.

MY HARD WORK WILL BRING
ME GREAT REWARDS.

Proverbs 14:23 (NIV) – All hard work brings profit, but mere talk leads only to poverty.

"Hard work pays off!" This is a familiar adage that resonates with many of us. The Bible is replete with scriptures affirming that God rewards diligence. This reward is not limited to our professional endeavors or businesses; it extends to every facet of our lives. Strive to excel as a son or daughter, as a spouse, as a parent, and in your relationship with God.

Colossians 3:23-24 exhorts us, "Whatever you do, work heartily, as for the Lord and not for men, knowing that from the Lord you will receive the inheritance as your reward. You are serving the Lord Christ." Let your actions reflect your devotion to God, not the accolades of this world, for ultimately, it is God who has the ultimate authority.

Philippians 2:14-15 encourages us to "Do all things without grumbling or disputing, that you may be blameless and innocent, children of God without blemish in the midst of a crooked and twisted generation, among whom you shine as lights in the world." Persist through the challenging seasons of life without yielding to despair. The tempests we face are transient, and brighter days lie ahead.

God is cognizant of your efforts. Persevere to attain the rewards He has in store for you. Galatians 6:9 reminds us, "And let us not grow weary of doing good, for in due season we will reap, if we do not give up." The path of righteousness may be arduous, especially when goodness seems unreciprocated, but remember that your recompense comes from God, not from man.

Philippians 4:13 (KJV) declares, "I can do all things through Christ which strengtheneth me." With the strength that God provides, you are capable of overcoming any obstacle. Your hard work will culminate in success. Keep going! Don't give up!

I WILL HUMBLE MYSELF.

James 4:10 (NIV) – Humble yourselves
before the Lord, and he will lift you up.

What does it mean to be humble? Christianity.com defines it as "recognizing our true selves as fallen in sin and utterly dependent on God." To see ourselves as we truly are is to acknowledge our imperfections and propensity to fall short. In our shortcomings, it is essential to humble ourselves, trusting that God will guide us in the right direction and teach us His ways. This is affirmed in Psalm 25:9-10 (NIV), which states, "He guides the humble in what is right and teaches them his way. All the ways of the Lord are loving and faithful toward those who keep the demands of his covenant."

Humility involves placing our complete trust in the Lord and His wisdom, knowing that He will never lead us astray. Proverbs 22:4 (KJV) offers a more explicit definition of humility: "By humility and the fear of the Lord are riches, and honor, and life." Humility is about recognizing God's greatness and the joy and peace that come from Him. Furthermore, Christianity.com emphasizes the significance of humility in acknowledging our flawed human nature on Earth and our vulnerability to sin if we are not vigilant against temptation:

> 1 Peter 5:8-11 says, "Be alert and of
> sober mind. Your enemy the devil prowls

around like a roaring lion looking for someone to devour. Resist him, standing firm in the faith, because you know that the family of believers throughout the world is undergoing the same kind of sufferings. And the God of all grace, who called you to his eternal glory in Christ, after you have suffered a little while, will himself restore you and make you strong, firm, and steadfast. To him be the power for ever and ever. Amen."

Humble yourself and trust that God will guide you through whatever challenges you face. Do not be overly proud or unaware of God's power. The Enemy prowls like a roaring lion, seeking to devour you. There's a modern saying, "If you know, you know (IYKYK)," which implies that when you know better, you do better. Keep going! Don't give up!

I WILL WRITE MY GOALS AND VISIONS AND PRIORITIZE WHAT IS IMPORTANT.

Luke 14:28-31 (NIV) – *Suppose one of you wants to build a tower. Won't you first sit down and estimate the cost to see if you have enough money to complete it? For if you lay the foundation and are not able to finish it, everyone who sees it will ridicule you, saying, 'This person began to build and wasn't able to finish.' Or suppose a king is about to go to war against another king. Won't he first sit down and consider whether he is able with ten thousand men to oppose the one coming against him with twenty thousand?*

Have you ever gone to the grocery store without writing out your list, only to get back home and realize you bought everything except what you intended to purchase? Or perhaps you have a lengthy To-Do list, and you attempt to rely on mental notes instead of writing it down. By the end of the day or week, you find that you've omitted some particularly important tasks because you forgot to write them down or prioritize them.

The same principle applies to our goals and aspirations. Writing our vision or goals helps us focus and prioritize our actions. Being obedient to what God wants us to do will bring blessings. Trusting in God's process, He will assist us in bridging the gaps needed to achieve our goals. When we commit our plans to paper, we must have faith that they will come to fruition. It may not come when we want it, but it will come right on time.

> Hebrews 11:1-3 (NIV) says, "Now faith is confidence in what we hope for and assurance about what we do not see. This is what the ancients were commended for. By faith we understand that the universe was formed at God's command, so that what is seen was not made out of what was visible."

Just because something has never been done does not mean it cannot be accomplished, and just because someone else has achieved it does not mean you cannot do it in your own unique way and appeal to a different audience. Don't hesitate to ask God, "What is Your vision for my life?"

Team Jesus Magazine advises, "Ask God what He wants to accomplish through you. His vision for our lives extends far beyond our understanding. Several scriptures remind us of this: Jeremiah 29:11 assures us that God knows the plans He has for us. Jeremiah 33:3 promises that if we call upon Him, He will reveal things we do not know. Proverbs 3:5-6 urge us to trust in Him and acknowledge Him in all our endeavors. His word promises that He will guide our steps. When we pray and fully surrender to His will, He can work wonders in our lives."

Keep going! Don't give up!

I WILL SPEAK ABOUT WONDERFUL THINGS IN MY LIFE.

Proverbs 18:21 (NIV) – The soothing tongue is a tree of life, but a perverse tongue crushes the spirit.

Words are powerful. Speak remarkable affirmations over your life. Examples include: "I can do it," "I will get through this," "I am strong," "I am beautiful," "I am smart," "I am a good person," "I deserve the great things God has planned for me," "I love who I am," "I am proud of myself," and the list goes on. Speak life, not death. Build yourself up, encourage yourself, and motivate yourself.

Proverbs 15:4 (NIV) says, "The soothing tongue is a tree of life, but a perverse tongue crushes the spirit." The words we utter lead to action. They originate in the heart before they are spoken by the tongue. When you tell yourself, "I am beautiful," and truly believe it, you will see no flaws when you look in the mirror.

You could have the biggest pimple of the year, and yet, God still seems to grant you all the confidence in the world. However, when you tell yourself, "I am ugly, and nobody likes me," you begin to feel depressed upon looking in the mirror. You don't want to see your reflection, then conceal your true self with superficial things. At the end of the day, when the Band-Aids are removed, a sense of emptiness remains; you still don't feel good about yourself because you have declared negativity over your life. It's a matter of cause and effect. If you convince yourself that you can't accomplish something, then you won't be able to do it.

According to Christianity.com, "A crushed spirit is a wounded soul within their emotions. A traumatized soul shuts down their emotions, essentially extinguishing them. Words that carry life can resurrect dead emotions through healing. You have a choice, and the matter of life and death has always involved making a choice. From the beginning, God has always offered humanity the option between life and death. In the Garden of Eden, He placed the tree of life and the tree of the knowledge of good and evil at the center to present the choice between life and death."

Choose life, not death! Keep going! Don't give up!

I WILL PRAY OFTEN.

John 15:7 (NIV) – If you remain in me and my words remain in you, ask whatever you wish, and it will be done for you.

Prayer is a means through which we communicate with God. He listens to us, and through prayer, we can bless not only ourselves but also our families and others.

When life is flourishing and God blesses us beyond our expectations, we should pray to express gratitude for our many blessings, seek humility, and ask that He continues to uplift us. Thank God for all He is doing in your life. When you find yourself at the lowest point, pray to God for all your needs with as much humility as you can muster. We should pray during both our highest highs and lowest lows because God oversees all things. Prayer ushers in peace, love, and joy into our lives and can enlighten us about God's plan and purpose for us. It aids in developing a relationship with God. Fostering this relationship allows us to hear from God more clearly through our thoughts, feelings, scriptures, and the actions of others.

Like any relationship, if it is not nurtured, it will not flourish. It becomes more challenging to hear from God when we are distant from Him. Prayer helps us comprehend that God is love, and love never fails. It clarifies the answers to our prayers. God will assist you in understanding your purpose and reason for existence.

Prayer guides you in finding direction and staying on the path that God has planned for you. It provides hope and strength to resist things that are not of God or to avoid temptations. Prayer aligns our desires with what God has planned for our lives. The purpose of prayer is not to dictate to God how He should act, but rather to help us understand who He is and to transform our actions accordingly. Through prayer, the Lord can perform miracles, such as forgiving sins, healing the sick, and bestowing the gifts of joy and peace. Prayer invites the Holy Spirit into our lives and helps us feel God's presence. While prayer does not alter God's plan for our lives, it transforms us. Keep going! Don't give up!

Even when times get tough, I will remain faithful to God.

Mark 4:31-32 (NIV) – It is like a mustard seed, which is the smallest of all seeds on earth. Yet when planted, it grows and becomes the largest of all garden plants, with such big branches that the birds can perch in its shade.

All you need is a little faith to begin your journey. Sometimes, getting started is the hardest part, but I encourage you to take that first step. Plant those seeds and watch them grow. I want to conclude this devotional with:

John 15:1-25 (NIV) "I am the true vine, and my father is the gardener. He cuts off every branch in me that bears no fruit, while every branch that does bear fruit, he prunes so that it will be even more fruitful. You are already clean because of the words I have spoken to you. Remain in me, as I also remain in you. No branch can bear fruit by itself; it must remain in the vine. Neither can you bear fruit unless you remain in me.

"I am the vine; you are the branches. If you remain in me and I in you, you will bear much fruit; apart from me you can do nothing. If you do not remain in me, you are like a branch that is thrown away and withers; such branches are picked up, thrown into the fire, and burned. If you remain in me and my words remain in you, ask whatever you wish, and it will be done for you. This is to my Father's glory, that you bear much fruit, showing yourselves to be my disciples.

"As the Father has loved me, so have I loved you. Now remain in my love. If you keep my commands, you will remain in my love, just as I have kept my Father's commands and remain in his love. I have told you this so that my joy may be in you and that your joy may be complete. My command is this: Love each other as I have loved you. Greater love has no one than this: to lay down one's life for one's friends. You are my friends if you do what I command. I no longer call you servants because a servant does not know his master's business. Instead, I have called you friends, for everything that I learned from my Father I have made known to you. You did not choose me, but I chose you and appointed you so that you might go and bear fruit—fruit that will last—and so that whatever you ask in my name the Father will give you. This is my command: Love each other.

"If the world hates you, keep in mind that it hated me first. If you belonged to the world, it would love you as its own. As it is, you do not belong to the world, but I have chosen you out of the world. That is why the world hates you. Remember what I told you: 'A servant is not greater than his master.' If they persecuted me, they would persecute you also. If they obeyed my teaching, they would obey yours also. They will treat you this way because of my name, for they do not know the one who sent me. If I had not come and spoken to them, they would not be guilty of sin; but now they have no excuse for their sin. Whoever hates me hates my Father as well. If I had not done among them the work no one else did, they would not be guilty of sin. As it is, they have seen, and yet they have hated both me and my Father. But this is to fulfill what is written in their Law: 'They hated me without reason.'"

Conclusion

God is good; God is faithful. Do not give up.

When life becomes challenging, when we grieve the loss of something or someone, we must persevere. Trust in Him. Believe in His Word. Cultivate a relationship with God so that He may grant you discernment—the ability to judge wisely and make sound decisions.

Joy and peace are gifts from God. When we encounter struggles or roadblocks and feel stuck, we should pray and depend on God. Trust in Him, and He will guide you through. Life is difficult, and tough times are inevitable, but the key lies in how we handle these challenges. Do not lose yourself during these times or succumb to heartbreak because you did not seek God's wisdom or rely on His Word. That is not God's desire for us! This is in accordance with the teachings of the Christian Church at Charleston Four Corners:

> "The Bible describes God as a Spirit and is the Creator of all things. He alone is eternal (has always existed) and is the self–existing one (He is completely

self–sufficient and independent of
anything else for His existence). He
is loving, all–knowing, all–powerful,
omnipresent (present everywhere at all
times), unchanging, holy (without sin),
just, long–suffering, gracious, righteous,
and merciful. He is the One True God
(all other so–called gods are nothing but
man–made idols) who reveals Himself in
three persons: God the Father, God the
Son, and God the Holy Spirit."

Have you struggled with grief and loss? Whether it's the
death of a loved one, losing a pet, the end of a friendship, a
divorce, or a life-altering illness or injury that has redefined
your daily life, losing a home, or unemployment—these
experiences can lead us to question whether God notices our
pain or if we've been forgotten. This 30-day devotional serves
as a reminder that, amidst grief and life's daily challenges, we
must not lose ourselves. It reassures us that God's presence is
constant, that we are not forgotten, and that there is a divine
purpose and plan for our lives. This book encourages us to
trust in God throughout our journey.

About the Author

Vanecia Codner was a devout woman of faith whose life was marked by service, joy, and an unwavering love for God. She poured her heart into children's ministry, serving as Sunday School Superintendent for the Children's Department at Metropolitan A.M.E. Zion Church in Kansas City, Missouri, and contributing her gifts to Evangel Church's children's ministry as well.

Beyond ministry, Vanecia was the cherished wife of Domingo Codner and the proud mother of Alex and Za'Nyla Codner. Her love for family and community was a true reflection of her faith in action.

This book is published posthumously, honoring the life God so beautifully shaped in her. Though she has taken her final walk home with Him, her spirit, wisdom, and devotion continue to speak through these pages. Her family treasures this work as a lasting legacy, an offering of encouragement, guidance, and inspiration for all who read it.